THE
PICTURESQUE
RAILWAY

Cover illustrations: *Front*: Avon Viaduct, Wolston, Warwickshire; *Rear*: The Maidenhead Bridge.

First published 2015

The History Press
The Mill, Brimscombe Port
Stroud, Gloucestershire, GL5 2QG
www.thehistorypress.co.uk

British Library Cataloguing in Publication Data.
A catalogue record for this book is available from the British Library.

ISBN 978 0 7509 6094 6

Typesetting and origination by The History Press
Printed and bound in Malta by Melita Press

THE PICTURESQUE RAILWAY

THE LITHOGRAPHS OF JOHN COOKE BOURNE

MATT THOMPSON

Contents

Acknowledgements

I would like to thank my colleagues at the Ironbridge Gorge Museum Trust, both past and present, for their help and support in the production of this book. In particular I would like to thank David de Haan, who has carried out a great deal of work on the subject of Bourne and his contemporaries.

As has been mentioned elsewhere in the book, John van Laun has been a great help in looking over the text and has of late added much to our knowledge of Bourne's work.

Ed Bartholomew at the National Railway Museum first introduced me to the work of Bourne and the picturing of the early railways. He has provided much scholarly support on these and many other subjects.

Finally I would like to thank my partner and my son, Harris, for their patience and for allowing me the space and quiet to work at home.

Preface

It is with some trepidation on my part that another railway book is produced to add to the many thousands published each year. Almost every aspect of the railways in Great Britain has been covered, some in great technical detail and others in more popular terms. Railways fascinate people; from an early period in their development the notions of classification, timetabling, organisation and structure seem to appeal to a wide audience. It is perhaps the fact that the railways lend themselves so readily to an idea of an ordered universe, one that can be described, documented and understood through the examination of its component parts that has proved its biggest attraction. On the other hand, it may just be because they look good; that they cut something of a dashing figure as they move through the landscape and that the idea of speeding through the countryside still holds a childlike excitement for many.

However, it is still something of a surprise to find that there are gaps in the subjects covered by all of these railway books. Of course, new research and new approaches to existing material will always mean that new gaps (unknown-unknowns as they might be called) are brought to light; but the work of John Cooke Bourne has been known about for the best part of 175 years and, in certain circles, his work has been admired and discussed alongside some of the greatest artists that ever lived (the great collector Sir Arthur Elton referred to him as the 'Piranesi of the age of steam'). So it is a surprise to find that his work was only reprinted once by David & Charles and that was over forty years ago. It is indicative of the quality of these facsimile editions that they are now considered highly collectable in their own right.

Bourne's images of the London & Birmingham Railway (L&BR) and the Great Western Railway (GWR) have captivated and inspired many generations of enthusiasts, historians and researchers and yet there has been no easy opportunity to see his work outside of small reproductions in books and magazines. Worse still, this means that an artist with prodigious talent has remained somewhat exclusive and it has been difficult to show his work to new audiences in the hope of inspiring them.

It is hoped that the present volume will fill this gap. It is not a particularly academic work, nor was it designed to be. It is unashamedly a picture book; it is all about giving the widest possible audience the chance to see and appreciate Bourne's work. The images in the present volume have been taken from contemporary lithographs contained within the Elton Collection which is held at the Ironbridge Gorge Museum Trust, Coalbrookdale. Sadly, space constraints mean that several lithographs from each volume have had to be overlooked for inclusion. Very often these have been the beautiful images of churches and church architecture that Bourne executed with such skill and accuracy. For these omissions I apologise.

The information not technical and may disappoint those who would like more detail about types of locomotives, rolling stock or the technology of signalling. The captions have been kept short and much of the information they contain has come from the contemporary text that accompanied the lithographs when they were first published in collected volumes. The introductory text is just that – an introduction. The histories of the L&BR and GWR have already been published in more detail than my own limited knowledge would allow.

Remaining with the subject of my own limited knowledge, I feel it only proper to mention here those who have gone before me and provided so much by way of information and references. Sir Arthur Elton and John Somers Cocks are two whose work I have read and enjoyed. I have had the pleasure of working alongside and benefiting from the extensive knowledge of David de Haan at Ironbridge. There are others who are working towards the goal of having the work of John Cooke Bourne more widely recognised. These include Ed Bartholomew at the National Railway Museum, and John Van Laun, who has produced a detailed series of articles on Bourne for the Railway and Canal Historical Society's *Journal*.

I sincerely hope that this book is both enjoyable and informative. Images such as these can bring the past to life in a way that is more direct and accessible than any text. The Industrial Revolution was not undertaken in rooms full of clerks and secretaries; it was physical, outdoors, vital and, for want of a better term, a messy affair. Bourne's lithographs capture that strength and dynamism in a way that words alone cannot.

Introduction

Railways: a brief overview up to the 1830s

The railways were born in the mines of central Europe in the fifteenth century and were essentially tracks consisting of wooden planks laid with a small gap between them on which a truck with small, wide wheels ran. A strong pin projected from the bottom of the truck and ran in the gap between the planks meaning that the truck could be pushed along in near-total darkness without derailing. This technology is likely to have arrived in Great Britain in the mid 1560s and it was quickly adapted for use outside of a mine situation.

The earliest surviving reference to a surface railway is from 1603 and records a short line at Wollaton, Nottinghamshire. In 1605–08, the proceedings of a series of court cases record a railway and an inclined plane already in use at Broseley, near the Severn Gorge, Shropshire. These early wooden railways were all designed to overcome the problems associated with moving large quantities of heavy materials, in this case coal, from mines to navigable rivers or to the coast where it could be shipped longer distances by sea. With the exception of stretches constructed by the Romans, the roads in Britain were extremely difficult to operate on. In summer they could be dusty and hard while for the rest of the year they were often boggy and impassable. Landowners despaired of packhorses and wagons that swerved to avoided rutted areas, as this would widen the road to an enormous size and ruin potentially productive farmland. The railway, a simple set of wooden rails on which a cart with flanged wheels ran, meant that a more permanent way could be established that could operate effectively, regardless of the weather or ground conditions.

Throughout the seventeenth century an increasing, albeit small, number of lines were built, particularly in coalfields such as those around Newcastle upon Tyne, around the River Wear and East Shropshire. The development was not a smooth progress as the turbulent period of the Civil Wars and the Commonwealth appear to have had a significant impact on the development of the railways. However, by the eighteenth century, horse-drawn railways were becoming more commonplace in those areas where the extractive industries were based.

As the Industrial Revolution developed it became clear that the movement of raw materials, fuel and finished goods was fundamental to a flourishing economy; it was because of this that navigable rivers and subsequently the canal network were developed. While, in broad terms, the railways predated the canal network, they were often used solely as feeder lines leading from a colliery or mine to a canal wharf. Being in the main horse-drawn, their abilities to physically haul the quantities of material necessary to be economical were limited and waterborne transport was still far more effective over longer distances. There were, however, some significant developments in railway technology in this period. In 1729, the Coalbrookdale Company, Shropshire, cast the first iron railway wagon wheels, and later, in 1767, iron plates were fitted to the upper surfaces of the wooden rails at Coalbrookdale, a development that would later lead to the solid iron rail.

However, alongside the development of the canals and the horse-drawn railway the stationary steam engine was being perfected, used for pumping water, providing a blast for furnaces and drawing up and lowering men and materials in mines. By the 1790s engineers in Britain were beginning to experiment with using such steam engines to power road vehicles. These experiments met with mixed results but they sowed the seeds of using steam power as a means of locomotion. In 1802–03, once again at Coalbrookdale, experiments were made with a steam-powered railway locomotive. It seems that these were only partially successful and that the locomotive was left unfinished. One of those involved in the experiments, and who perhaps had the leading hand in them, was the engineer Richard Trevithick, who went on to build the first truly successful working steam locomotive in 1804.

Matters progressed quickly as the enquiring minds of the engineers sought to develop more effective and efficient steam locomotives. But, in these early years, the idea of a steam locomotive having a truly radical impact on the world appears to have been overlooked. In terms of 'polite' society the steam locomotive was very much a novelty in the early 1800s, as can be seen by Trevithick's use of a locomotive as something of a tourist attraction. His *Catch Me Who Can* locomotive of 1808 ran on a circular track in London and rides were offered to the public at a shilling a time.

After Trevithick's early successes with steam locomotion several other engineers began to design and build steam-powered locomotives to work at collieries around the country. These included names such as George Stephenson, Timothy Hackworth and John Blenkinsop. Up to this point the railways had been the exclusive preserve of mining and heavy industry and had been used to move goods, not people, but the spirit of the age was experimentation and speculation, and it was not long before the notion of a steam railway for the conveyance of passengers began to be mooted. Equally, up to the early 1820s, such was the lack of confidence in the reliability of the early steam locomotives that railways had been built to use a mixture of both mechanical and horse power.

In 1821 an Act of Parliament was passed which incorporated the Stockton & Darlington Railway (S&DR), which served the collieries of County Durham. The father-and-son team of George and Robert Stephenson had resurveyed the route and also recommended that it should be worked with steam locomotives as opposed to horses. While there were already many small railways in the North East this one, when opened, was the first public railway, insofar as it was not privately owned and operated by the colliery. It followed the usual model of running from colliery to port but, for the first time, it also allowed passengers to be carried as well.

The eyes, minds and perhaps most importantly the pockets of the industrialists and investors were opened by the success of the S&DR, and a slew of other railway companies sought, and were granted, an Act of Parliament between 1824 and 1826. Among them was the Liverpool & Manchester Railway (L&MR). The transatlantic cotton trade saw raw cotton shipped into Liverpool before being transported, by waterway, to the mills of Manchester. The canals, while a significant improvement on the roads at the time, were considered to be both inefficient and monopolistic and goods could take a significant time to reach the mills and be converted both into fabric and profits. The first proposed railway connecting the two cities was defeated in Parliament in 1825 by a combination of landowners and canal owners but, when resubmitted in 1826, an Act was granted and George Stephenson was appointed as engineer.

The Liverpool & Manchester Railway was opened on 15 September 1830 by the Prime Minister, the Duke of Wellington (who had personal reservations about the benefits that railways would bring). Despite an accident on the first day which saw the death of William Huskisson MP, the L&MR went on to have unexpected success with its passenger services. By 1831 the L&MR carried around 15,000 passengers in a single summer.

The L&MR was the first intercity railway but many more were to follow it, not least the London & Birmingham Railway (L&BR) and the Great Western Railway (GWR) that figure so large in this book. From its humble origins as a means of moving trucks safely in the dark confines of the central Europe mines, the railway was set to transform the world. Travelling times were cut almost unimaginably and places that had once been considered far apart were now within easy reach of each other. Throughout the 1830s and '40s the railways in Great Britain grew exponentially in what became known as the Railway Mania. However, even once that bubble had burst there was still an appetite for more railway building. It was in this world of excitement and experimentation that John Cooke Bourne grew up and his record of the feats of engineering that he saw are testaments to the achievements of his times.

John Cooke Bourne: His Early Life and Railway Lithographs

Bourne was by no means the first artist to capture the railways, either under construction or in operation. As a phenomenon, the railways had always attracted intense levels of interest from those who encountered them. From the woodcuts of Agricola's *De Re Metallica* of 1556 to the engraving of the railway at Prior Park in 1752, the artist's imagination and eye had been caught by this new way of moving through the landscape.

As the eighteenth century moved on railways began to appear in a number of engravings, often almost incidentally or in the background, but it was in the nineteenth century that the railway began to be pictured more and more prominently. Railways were, for a time, a real novelty and something that many people wanted to see. For those who worked in the collieries, mines and wharves where railways were built, they quickly became a commonplace feature of everyday life. For those who were keeping abreast of the latest developments in science, technology and indeed culture, they were of huge interest.

In September 1814, Britain was beginning to be aware of the great possibilities that lay ahead. Across the country developments were taking place that would have a profound effect on the lives of those who would go on to shape the nineteenth century. The Industrial Revolution, and all the precipitous social and economic change that went along with it, was gaining momentum. On the Continent Napoleon Bonaparte had been exiled to Elba, ending the first of the Napoleonic Wars, while in North America British troops were fighting what was known as the War of 1812 against the Americans and their allies in a conflict that would last more than two and a half years.

It was in July of that year that the engineer George Stephenson trialled a steam locomotive at the Killingworth Colliery near Newcastle upon Tyne. This locomotive, *Blücher* (named after a Prussian general) performed relatively well. The railways were very much in their infancy and Stephenson, along with others at the time, was keen to demonstrate that a locomotive with smooth wheels could actually be effective on

Prior Park, the Seat of Ralph Allen Esq. near Bath, 1752.

smooth track; many thought the addition of a rack and cog system essential to any viable operation. His experiment proved successful, although the power of the machine was still questionable. The very basic assumptions on which the railways would be founded were being worked out at this time by mechanics, engineers and blacksmiths. A new way of moving through the landscape was being developed and it is likely that none of those involved at this point would have had any awareness of just how profound their influence would be.

It was into this world of international conflict and domestic experimentation that, on 1 September 1814, John Cooke Bourne was born at 19 Lamb's Conduit Street, London, to Edward, a hatter, and Mary Ann. John was to become a chronicler of some of the most impressive feats of engineering of the nineteenth century. He was to be perhaps the first artist to capture in detail the work that went into building the greatest monuments of the age: the railways.

In their London residence, the Bourne family were closely linked to a family with prodigious artistic talent, the Cookes. George Cooke and his brother William were engravers of some note; both brothers had engraved the work of the artist J.W.M. Turner among many other commissions. Family tradition had it that George Cooke was the godfather of John Cooke Bourne and that his middle name reflected this strong familial bond. However, the fact that John's father also had the middle name of Cooke suggests that whatever relationship existed between them was longstanding.

Whatever the details of the bond between the two families, the influence of the Cooke family must have been strong because from an early age John Cooke Bourne's artistic ability was spotted, nurtured and developed.

In 1828, aged 14, John was apprenticed to another well-known engraver, John Pye. In common with the Cooke brothers, Pye had also engraved many works by Turner and it is perhaps this professional connection that enabled the apprenticeship to be arranged. Bourne's early sketches show a great deal of Pye's influence but also demonstrate the eye for detail that would mark out his later railway lithographs as being something exceptional. The topographical tradition that portrayed landscapes, picturesque ruins and sublime castles and crags suffused Bourne's early work. These were aesthetic traditions established in the eighteenth century that were still popular in the early nineteenth, but they were obviously not enough to keep the young artist satisfied.

But Bourne was not to be starved of inspiration for long. By 1836 the landscape of London was beginning to be radically transformed by the coming of the railways. The L&BR was cutting a swathe through the capital. These excavations, which were so memorably captured in prose by Charles Dickens in his novel *Dombey and Son*, were busy, noisy, dirty affairs with the harsh ring of picks against stone and the shouts of surveyors, foremen and the navigators (themselves brought together from all over the United Kingdom) mingling into an unfamiliar cacophony. Bourne visited these sites and sketched them, capturing the birth of the first mainline railway in the world and, perhaps more importantly, documenting the everyday lives of those whose work helped to transform the nation. His sketches from this period are full of life and movement. In a world as yet without a practically useful form of photography his well-observed drawings are honest and without guile. They show not only the men at work but snatching brief periods of leisure, they show the animals that lived and worked alongside the men, and they show the enormous scale of the work involved in building a railway, essentially by hand.

His work was noticed by John Britton, a publisher who had worked closely with Bourne's master John Pye on a number of illustrative projects. Britton stated that Bourne's motivation for making the initial drawings had been *con amore* – simply for the love of it – but he was convinced that there would be a market for images such as these and he encouraged Bourne to develop his sketches into fully worked-up drawings and, from these, lithographic prints. A whole series of line-and-wash drawings were produced, around fifty in total, with thirty-six eventually being published by Britton in 1838 and '39. Although they were originally made available in a series of part-works at one guinea each they must have

Sketch of workers on the L&BR. The note to the bottom right reads '3 days or more on this', indicating the time required to finish the stone.
John Cooke Bourne, 1837.

sold well, as a collected volume was published later in 1839, under the title *Drawings of the London & Birmingham Railway.*

It is worthwhile noting that the railways were not to everyone's taste and that, from the outset, there was a strategic, if not political, element to Bourne's work as published by Britton. Bourne's lithographs of the L&BR were collectively published with accompanying text by Britton which covered the history of railways to that date, details on the construction of the line and notable landscapes and locations that could be seen along the railway. As part of his research for this text Britton wrote to the secretary of the L&BR, Richard Creed, asking for information that he could include. At the end of the letter he stated:

> Fully aware that we have jealous & fastidious critics to deal with both in the houses of parliament [*sic*] & out of them, I wish to remove, or at least to check, the tide of prejudice against us, and display our powers, capabilities and effects.

Many landowners, who were also members of Parliament, were set against the railways for a number of reasons. There were anxieties about the erosion of the social order and the ability for the working classes to move freely around the country; there were concerns surrounding sharp financial practices and the sale of shares; but, perhaps foremost in the minds of many of the landowning classes was the detrimental effect that the railways would have on their carefully landscaped estates and the potentially negative impact on their ability to hunt.

Bourne's work was a combination of the picturesque, topographical style that was seen as acceptable to the landowning classes and the technically accurate penmanship of an industrial draughtsman. As such, his work framed the sometimes shocking newness of the railways in an aesthetic that was familiar and reassuring to those who felt its initial inconveniences (and, it must not be forgotten, subsequent financial recompense) most keenly.

Quite what the actual effect of Bourne's images of the building of the L&BR had on the landowning classes at the time is difficult to gauge accurately, although a list of subscribers to his work on the L&BR contains some extremely prominent names, such as Lord Wharncliffe who would go on to have a pivotal role to play in the GWR's campaign for royal assent. However, reviewers of his work in the popular press were more vocal. The *Gentleman's Magazine* of October 1839 stated that Bourne had 'secured credit to himself … by the accuracy and spirit of his delineations' and that he would 'speedily rank among the first landscape painters of our age'.

The late 1830s and early 1840s constituted a period of railway building that grew to be known as the Railway Mania. In 1830 there were just over 97 miles of railway open in Britain out of a total of 349 miles that had been sanctioned by Act of Parliament. By 1835 there were 337 miles opened for traffic out of 970 miles sanctioned. By 1840, just one year after Bourne's work on the L&BR had been published in its entirety, this had grown to 1,497 miles of railway open out of a staggering 2,553 miles sanctioned. The number of railway companies seeking an Act of Parliament increased dramatically as railways came to be seen as *the* commodity to invest in. What began in 1825 and 1826 as a 'railway fever' soon grew to a panic in the 1830s, as increasing numbers of lines were proposed and shares in these speculative ventures began to be traded in larger quantities, and then by the mid 1840s to a full-grown mania. Investors, large and small, were persuaded to buy into railway schemes of all kinds. Some were meeting a clear transport need and greatly improved upon the existing roads and canals, but others were foolish flights of fancy projecting railways along routes which had little or no chance of turning a profit had they managed to negotiate the arduous and extremely expensive process of obtaining royal assent.

It was into this febrile world of railway enthusiasm that Bourne's initial works were published. For the next few years Bourne produced a small number of railway lithographs and, working from the drawings of others, illustrated a number of books. It is also known that he spent some time at Woburn Abbey and produced a series of watercolours of the abbey when it was visited by Queen Victoria in 1841. However, by 1843, Bourne had been approached by another major figure in publishing, Charles Cheffins. Following on from the success of the lithographs of the L&BR, Cheffins commissioned Bourne to document the GWR, which was then under construction, having being given royal assent in 1835. In addition to commissioning the work, Cheffins offered to finance the publication of the final volume in its entirety.

Bourne's lithographs of the GWR were first published, in an extremely short run, in 1843; it took a further three years for *The History and Description of the Great Western Railway* to appear. The images were far more confident and assured and contained perhaps less documentary rawness than his images of the L&BR. While the navvies do appear in several of the images, the GWR is pictured far more as a finished product, as indeed it was by 1843. These were more a triumphant testament to the skills of Brunel and his engineers than a piece of 1830s reportage about the changing face of the countryside. There is a move towards an even greater picturesque, even pastoral, feel to the images. This is in contrast to the images of the L&BR, which could be described more by way of the aesthetic concept of the sublime, or awe-inspiring, qualities of the railway, rather than the picturesque. With his lithographs of the GWR, Bourne demonstrated his ability to capture a railway that, although brand new, was already at home in the British countryside.

But the railway world was changing; by 1846 the Railway Mania was at its peak but it had already begun to claim its first victims as fortunes, both small and large, were lost on the share markets. The number of railway bills that had received royal assent in that year allowed for a total of more than £95 million to be raised through the sale of shares, and there was no shortage of buyers. But these investors were often buying shares in schemes that were little more than an attractive pamphlet advertising the speculative potential of the railway in question. In all too many cases the scheme did not progress any further forward than a purely paper exercise but, by that time, the shareholders' money would have been spent on surveyors costs and legal fees. Very quickly the public attitude towards the railways started to move from overheated enthusiasm to mistrust and disdain.

All of this meant that, in 1846, an expensive volume of railway lithographs was not perhaps the most popular of books. Although Bourne's talent was clear to see and the railways, as a subject, provided a huge range of possibilities for interesting and exciting compositions, Bourne did not go on to produce any more volumes of lithographs as he had for the L&BR and GWR. His first work had been triumphant and had captured the pioneering engineering and financial speculations of the late 1830s while his second had captured a major railway already settled into the landscape and operating in harmony with the hamlets, villages and towns through which it passed. But this later work was, by the time of its appearance, sadly out of step with the majority of public opinion. In all Bourne had captured perhaps the most exciting and tumultuous ten years in the history of the railways. In this short period fortunes were made and lost, landscapes and towns altered, sometimes beyond recognition, and the ability of people and goods to move around the country was radically transformed. Bourne managed to record all of this and the influence of his work has been felt down through the years.

1

The London & Birmingham Railway

In 1825 the Stockton & Darlington Railway (S&DR) opened to traffic in the North East of England. Developed out of the colliery railways that had been in existence in the local area for centuries, the S&DR forced landowners, speculators and investors up and down the country to take notice of the railways and their potential to dramatically transform the ways in which both goods and people were moved. In January 1824, just one year after the Act of Parliament allowing the use of steam locomotives on the S&DR, Sir John Rennie and Francis Giles began to survey two possible routes for a railway connecting London with Birmingham; one via Oxford and the other via Coventry.

A clear need for such a railway had been demonstrated by the rapid expansion of industrial activities in the Midlands. Local manufacturers in and around Birmingham had found that, by the 1820s, they sometimes had to refuse orders because they simply could not move finished goods to the capital quickly enough. While small articles could be moved over the roads, large and heavy items such as those produced in the ironworks in the Midlands had to be transported on the canal system. It was a journey of three days to get material from Birmingham to London by canal and in poor conditions this could be even longer. In addition to this, as industry in the Midlands expanded it required ever more in terms of raw materials from outside of the area which again put strain on the canal network.

There was much rivalry between the two proposed routes but, ultimately, a line running via Coventry was decided upon and the two concerns were in effect amalgamated by 1830.

At this time George and Robert Stephenson were appointed to be the surveyors and refined the route while also providing an estimate of costs for construction. In 1832, the first share prospectus was issued with the capital needed to build the 112½ miles of double-track railway put at £2.5 million. The potential profits for the railway were put at more than £670,000 per year with the operating costs set to be less than half of that amount. Despite these attractive figures and the assent of the House of Commons, the Act of Parliament necessary to begin work was thrown out of the House of Lords in 1832. While there was a clear need for the railway to improve the industrial performance of the nation, there was a also a great deal of anxiety and antipathy towards the railways among the large landowners, the majority of whom also sat in the House of Lords. The fear was that the railways would spoil productive agricultural land, cut estates in two and, for some most importantly, seriously impact on the ability to ride to hounds over open country in pursuit of fox and deer.

Undeterred, a series of measures were introduced to calm the fears of the landowning classes. In broad terms, this amounted to the allocation of £250,000 to compensate landowners for the loss of land. It has been suggested that, in certain cases, £350 per acre was paid to secure land on which to build the railway, far in excess of the market rates at the time. Whatever the measures introduced, the bill was reintroduced to Parliament and received royal assent on 6 May 1833.

Once the Act of Parliament authorising the railway had been passed, work began on the construction. Land was purchased with the money raised from the sale of shares and contracts were made for the building works. The railway was built in a series of stages and, as each stage was completed, it was opened to limited services. Thus, rather than having a single 'grand opening' that, in a stroke, slashed the journey time between the capital and the nation's second city there was a gradual, inexorable joining together of towns along the route.

It had initially been planned that the London end of the railway would terminate at Camden Town but it was thought that this was too far from the centre of the capital and so, in 1835, an additional Act of Parliament was sought to allow for an extension to the railway into the heart of London at Euston. In order to bring the railway into the metropolis it was necessary to negotiate a steep 1 in 70 incline down from Camden to the city centre. It was decided that this was too steep for the locomotives of the day to travel upon and so a large engine house was constructed and the trains were lowered down and hauled up the line for the first 1¼ miles from Euston on cables wound by a large stationary steam engine at Camden. It was not until 1844 that steam locomotives became powerful enough to replace this method of setting out on the journey to Birmingham.

The first section to be completed and opened was from Euston to Boxmoor in July 1837; this was extended to Tring in October of the same year. By April 1838 the L&BR was able to transport passengers from London right through to Birmingham, although it must be stated that for 35 miles of this journey passengers had to travel by coach along the roads. It was five months later, on 17 September 1838, that the company's trains were first able to travel along the entire length of the railway.

The actual cost of construction was far in excess of the original estimate; in fact, costs totalled more than £5.5 million or just over £50,000 per mile of railway built. However, the journey time between the two cites was cut dramatically. What had previously taken three days by canal or eleven hours by stagecoach was now achievable in just six hours (although the mail train, which did not stop at any intermediate stations, could do it in five).

The L&BR, like all railways, evolved out of a need to move large, heavy items around the country with the minimum of effort and expense; this was certainly one of the prime motivations for proposing the railway in the first place. The completed railway fulfilled existing business needs exceptionally well. But it also helped to create another. The L&BR, due to its length and capacity, was the first truly main line railway in the world and its capacity to move people across large distances relatively quickly and in relative comfort was quickly recognised. In the first six months of operating, the L&BR carried just under 220,000 passengers and generated more than £160,000 in revenue for the company, compared to just over £10,400 in goods moved by rail over similar distances.

The building of the L&BR was an undertaking the scale of which had never been seen before. Its impact on the countryside was huge, although the railway quickly settled into its surroundings and its coming was perhaps less traumatic than was initially feared by farmers and landowners. Similarly, it also had a lasting impact on the urban townscape. London, Rugby, Coventry and Birmingham were all shaped by the railway as were the many smaller towns and villages along the route. The landscape through which the railway passed was being radically transformed, not just in physical terms but also in terms of the ability of people to move through it.

It was important for the L&BR to make a statement with its London terminus. Their station at Euston Square was sited to ensure it was both 'convenient and commodious' for passengers and goods. The company purchased a large parcel of land from the Duke of Bedford and the station, designed by Philip Hardwick, was constructed in the space of nine months.

The station itself was relatively small when first built but was separated from the street by a 300ft-long range of buildings comprised of a huge Doric gateway, or propylaeum, flanked by two lodges. At the time of construction it was considered that this gateway was on a far grander scale than had been attempted previously in this style. It stood over 72ft in height and both radically changed and dominated the London skyline in 1837 when it was constructed.

Bourne captures not only the grandeur and architectural severity of the gateway and its lodge houses but also depicts the station as a centre of social activity. People and carriages are flocking towards the station through the propylaeum and the decorative iron gates between the lodges. This image suggests the potential greatness of the railway company; although a new enterprise, the L&BR adopted ancient architectural principles to suggest its solidity and permanence. To this Bourne has added what the railways were most keen to attract: people. He has integrated the station, a massive new monument to industry and innovation, with the city and the people of London. He shows the station, not as some stately home situated in private parkland away from the general population, but as a public space created, in some sense at least, for the public good as well as for the benefit of shareholders.

Building Retaining Wall etc. near Park Street, Camden Town

Charles Dickens, in *Dombey and Son*, memorably described the L&BR's inexorable advance into the heart of London:

> The first shock of a great earthquake had, just at that period, rent the whole neighbourhood to its centre. Traces of its course were visible on every side. Houses were knocked down; streets broken through and stopped; deep pits and trenches dug in the ground; enormous heaps of earth and clay thrown up ... fragments of unfinished walls and arches and piles of scaffolding, and wildernesses of bricks[.]
>
> In short, the yet unfinished and unopened Railroad was in progress; and, from the very core of all this dire disorder, trailed smoothly away, upon its mighty course of civilisation and improvement.

Dickens, who lived only a short distance from Euston station, was writing after the fact in the mid 1840s, but Bourne spent a great deal of time sketching the construction of the line through London in September 1836. This image contrasts the relative calm and order of the Georgian houses of Camden Town with the apparent chaos of the building works. This image shows the railway in different stages of completion; in the middle distance is a finished road bridge while to the right can be seen an almost complete retaining wall. But this smoothness and regularity is offset by the rough excavations seen to the left of the picture. This dramatic and dynamic image is completed by a cast of hundreds of workmen – navvies – who captured Bourne's imagination, as can be seen in the many sketches he made of such men at work on the railway.

Hampstead Road Bridge

The construction of the railway was not solely concerned with making the permanent way for the locomotives and trains that were to follow. As much as any railway connects people and places, it also has the power to separate them and cut across existing roads and routes. This was especially true of the L&BR when building the line into London. A great deal of care and attention was given to ensuring that, wherever possible, the railway did not permanently sever pre-existing connections within the capital.

A similar amount of attention was given over to the design of the many road bridges that had to be constructed to ensure that routes remained open. The inclusion of some of these bridges in the finished work could be seen as an attempt on the part of the L&BR to reassure people that the building of a railway need not mean a curtailing of their other ways of moving around the city.

Whatever the reason, Bourne recorded a significant number of bridges of various types and designs built by the L&BR. In this image the Hampstead Road Bridge is seen under construction. It is typical of Bourne's work that the bridge is depicted in a half-finished state. The elegance of the design can still be clearly made out but the smooth, clean lines of the bridge and the retaining wall on the right are juxtaposed with the rubble to the left and the gang of workers, seen through the tunnel, working on the retaining walls beyond the bridge. This contrasting of the rough with the smooth and the tempering of the new with apparent disorder and decay is something that William Gilpin, eighteenth-century proponent of the notions of the sublime and picturesque, would surely have approved of.

It would be a mistake to think that the coming of the railways immediately made the canals obsolete; these two modes of transport coexisted, in one form or another, for several centuries. However, the construction of intercity railways from the mid 1820s to the 1850s meant that the relationship between the two had to be, to some degree, formalised as the relative advantages and disadvantages of each became clearer.

In 1837, when Bourne made the sketches for this image, the canals were still an essential part of the industrial infrastructure of the country. Indeed, Bourne depicts barges of various types off-loading material for the construction of the railway itself. This implies the close relationship between the two at the time. The canalside is teeming with people apparently unloading the barges and making their way back to the construction site along a series of raised barrow runs. In the midst of all this activity can be seen a figure in a black coat and black stovepipe hat, perhaps a bargeman or overseer, seated, calmly surveying the prospect before him. Bourne's depiction of the working man is one of his strengths and such discreet cameos lend an air of authenticity to his portrayal of the scene.

The bridge that Bourne has captured here is the first example of a suspension bridge built specifically for railway use and was considered 'one of the boldest specimens of construction on the line'. The deck of the bridge was suspended on iron bars attached to the curved iron ribs on each side of the bridge.

Building the Stationary Engine House, Camden Town

Coming out of Euston Station and into Camden Town, the incline of the railway was such that it was thought locomotives would not be able to haul the train reliably. It was therefore decided that a stationary engine would be constructed which would haul the train up what was known as Camden Bank on a rope more than 3,700 yards long. At the top of the bank the rope would be unhitched and the train would be coupled to a locomotive for the remainder of its journey. To house the stationary engine, a massive, vaulted structure was constructed by Robert Stephenson & Co.

Bourne captured the huge scope and scale of the construction of the stationary engine house in this lithograph. The vaults themselves can be seen in various stages of construction with wooden formers being planked over, and subsequently bricked over, or being lifted into place. Lines of hod carriers can be seen bringing bricks onto the site in a scene that today might seem more in keeping with the building of the pyramids in Egypt. In amongst all of this activity can be seen a surveyor and a small group of frock-coated gentlemen.

Ever mindful about locating the railway in some form of context, Bourne has included the buildings of Camden town in the distance, to the left of the image. That the railway is being built through, and at times directly over, a landscape that is already lived-in is a key aspect of his work. While surveyors, such as those pictured in this image, might draw lines on maps indicating the most advantageous route from one location to another, Bourne's work reminds the viewer that the railway was a project that impacted directly on the people who lived and worked along the route.

Locomotive Engine House

In this image can be seen the chimneys of the stationary engine house and the locomotive engine shed. It gives the sense of a truly 'railway landscape' being developed. The sidings, yards and structures that are glimpsed from train windows in the twenty-first century when pulling into towns and cities all have their roots in a scene such as this.

Bourne's eye for technical detail is very much to the fore as the lithograph has been annotated to provide brief descriptions of some of the track and associated mechanisms. He labels both the structures and also the winding gear for switching the points. It is important to bear in mind that such things were very novel in the late 1830s and required a level of explanation that would perhaps not be necessary today.

Camden Town Depot: Entrance Gateway to Locomotive Engine House

The Camden Town depot was over three-quarters of an acre in extent and was proudly proclaimed as being 'entirely fire proof'. It contained offices, warehouses, store rooms and, remarkably, accommodation for cattle. However, in this image Bourne has chosen to focus on the new beast of burden for the industrial age: the locomotive.

The locomotive is a 2-2-0 type and was built by Mather, Dixon and Company to a design by Edward Bury. These early locomotives had no cab to protect the driver and fireman and had a distinctive domed firebox. To the right of the image can be seen a worker winding the mechanism to move the points. This was before such time as signal boxes and automation and it gives a sense of the level of manual labour required to operate a railway in the early years.

Primrose Hill Tunnel

Accompanying Bourne's lithographs was a textual commentary by John Britton which described the line and the features of interest along it. When referring to the Primrose Hill Tunnel he stated that this 'subterranean channel, of utter darkness, usually excites strong anxieties and terrors in the timid mind' before reassuring the reader that the tunnel was perfectly safe.

Bourne's image of the mouth of the tunnel shows the classical influences on both the tunnel mouth and the retaining wing walls. The use of large long-and-short quoins and decorative finials give the structure the feel of an eighteenth-century country house; in this way the architecture of the railways was aping the building styles of the landowners through whose estates the line would pass. By employing the same aesthetic as the landed gentry it appears as if the railway was attempting to make itself more amenable to those who sometimes had the power to halt its progress, or at least, ensure that things could be made considerably more difficult.

View of the Watford Embankment

Once outside of London, Bourne's topographical style began to come into its own. This image shows the embankment and viaduct over the River Colne to the east of Watford. The embankment was 40ft high and over three-quarters of a mile in length. On the slopes of the embankment can be seen navvies who, in total, moved more than 1 million cubic metres of earth to build it.

The train is dwarfed by the embankment and has been very much swallowed up by the landscape itself. To the left of the picture can be seen the water meadows of the Colne with cattle grazing peacefully against a backdrop of willow trees.

Bourne has made clever use of distance in this lithograph. The railway, and those working on it, feel insignificant and could almost be overlooked by a casual observer, while in the foreground stone blocks, perhaps used in the building of the line, echo the depictions of classical ruins of Greece and Rome. This image frames the railway in terms of the picturesque landscape developed in the eighteenth century.

Colne Viaduct near Watford

COLNE VIADUCT near WATFORD. Sept 1837.

Appearing in the landscape almost like a Roman aqueduct, the viaduct over the Colne is pictured as a clean, white modern structure. Surrounding the viaduct are sheep and cattle that appear to be grazing peacefully. In the 1830s there was a great deal of concern about how the railways might frighten farm animals and impact on milk production.

Throughout Bourne's lithographs it is clear to see that he is attempting to calm the anxieties of those who were worried that the railway would spell an end to their way of life.

Watford Tunnel Face

This image shows the final phases of the construction of Watford Tunnel. This tunnel was bored through chalk, gravel and sand for a length of just over a mile. The chalk was relatively stable but the gravel and sand were exceptionally loose. In one tragic accident, ten men lost their lives while digging the tunnel after they were buried alive by 'a rush of sand and gravel through an opening in the chalk'. The company spent a great deal of time digging a secondary shaft to retrieve the bodies.

A wooden scaffold can be seen erected directly in front of the tunnel mouth and Bourne has pictured several men working here. The main crossbeam of the scaffold is bowing alarmingly and is another sign that the work of the navvy was dangerous in the extreme.

The size of the cutting in which the tunnel portal sits dwarfs the workmen and gives an impressive sense of scale to the work. In places the building of the railway reshaped the landscape and Bourne is at pains to demonstrate how big an undertaking this was. The short train of wagons in the foreground is being drawn by horse and is a reminder of how important the horse was in the early days of railway construction.

Nash Mill Bridge

This image again shows both canal and railway. After leaving Watford Tunnel and running for some miles over an embankment, the railway crossed the Grand Junction Canal which, at this point, ran along the route of the River Gade. The bridge was constructed of six large iron ribs and was a total of 66 yards in span.

Included in this image are several figures. To the right can be seen some men, or boys, fishing. This would imply that the canal was relatively clean although such figures were often added to images for picturesque effect. To the left is a pair of figures, perhaps a courting couple, who give the scene an air of intimacy amidst the stark modernity of the railway. In mid-stream a barge is working its way along the canal.

This is one of the most powerful images of the L&BR produced by Bourne. A massive embankment is being constructed, entirely by muscle power, with material being moved from a nearby cutting and then taken up on what are referred to as 'horse-runs'. A series of horses were harnessed to ropes that ran through pulleys and down planks to the base of the embankment. As each horse moved along the line of the embankment it pulled a barrow up along the plank. In this way heavy loads could be raised to the necessary height.

This method was extremely dangerous as the barrows themselves could become unstable due to the horse not pulling in a regular manner. The navvy, rather than supporting the barrow in the upward journey, was simply being carried along by it which meant that if the barrow came loose or was about to tip over he had to quickly gauge which side was safest to leap to avoid being crushed. In many cases the navvy would come bounding down the ramp with the barrow running after him. It was said that the navvies became so used to this that although each man had numerous accidents there was only ever one fatality from this.

View of a Cutting and Bridge near Berkhampstead

Following Boxmoor the railway ran through a cutting just to the north of Berkhamsted. A bridge over the railway is under construction and displays the same, somewhat alarming, scaffold as seen in previous images. The locomotive is hauling a short train of loaded wagons which possibly contain spoil from the building works themselves.

Everything that is 'railway' in this image is under construction and has been carefully balanced with aspects of the landscape that are settled and complete.

The buildings to the left are nestled into the woods and the church, depicted in such a clean, architectural manner, looks out over the whole scene. The view from the church tower of Berkhamsted would have changed radically during the 1830s; Bourne has pictured it as a solid and stable part of the countryside, apparently unaffected by the railway being built alongside it.

View of the Deep Cutting near Tring

While at first glance a very similar image to that of the embankment at Boxmoor, this image shows a very different piece of civil engineering – a cutting. Over 1.4 million cubic yards of earth were excavated in the construction of the cutting, which ran for 2½ miles at an average depth of 40ft. Again, horse-runs have been employed to aid the navvies in moving their barrows up the narrow ramps and the mechanism can be clearly seen to the left of the image. Bourne's use of perspective in this image helps to give a sense of scale to the excavation as the horse-runs can be seen disappearing off into the distance.

In excavating this cutting, workers uncovered several human skeletons along with pottery and 'antique urns'. The building of the railways in the mid-nineteenth century was a huge undertaking and one that uncovered significant quantities of archaeology. It is interesting to note that such discoveries were recorded in accounts of the building of the line, and the text shows a marked interest in the ancient landscapes through which the railway ran.

Now almost 35 miles from London the railway again crossed the Grand Junction Canal. In this instance it was by means of a five-ribbed iron bridge with a graceful, almost semi-circular, arch. Bourne has accentuated this graceful shape by reflecting it in the water of the canal. The clean lines of the bridge and the abutments that lead up to and away from it are softened by the trees and loose, sketchy style of the canal side.

The beauty of such bridges had been appreciated since 1779 when the Iron Bridge, the first architectural structure to be built entirely out of metal, was erected over the River Severn at Coalbrookdale.

Scene at Jackdaw Hill, near Linslade

After passing through Leighton Buzzard the railway entered a short tunnel before going through a cutting at the foot of Jackdaw Hill. The railway is almost entirely absent from this scene, which was included to demonstrate the 'character' of the landscape that the L&BR travelled through at this point. The publisher John Britton wrote that it was important to the railway to highlight the 'sylvan, romantic, and picturesque features' of the countryside it was moving through. However, in the distance, against a backdrop of exposed rock, navvies can be seen working away, presumably at the cutting.

Two barges can be seen on the canal, one is being towed by a horse while the other is moored up. Again, the free style of this image reflects Bourne's method of working. Rough sketches, made in the field, show that he captured much of the landscape quickly and with dynamism. Comparison between the sketches and the finished lithograph show that in many cases, little in the composition was altered in the studio.

Blasting the Rocks to Form an Excavate Passage, at Linslade

Before the advent of photography it was difficult to capture moments of drama with accuracy. In this case, Bourne has chosen to picture the precise point of detonation in the ongoing work of excavating the cutting near Linslade. The explosion is just to the right of centre and a great cloud of smoke is issuing from the rock face. The navvies, no doubt used to such explosions, are standing a short distance away and are apparently calm spectators, continuing with their conversations.

However, to the left of the explosion three figures, two women and a child, appear to be fleeing the scene in fear of their lives, hotly pursued by two small dogs. In this image Bourne has not only captured an instant in time, he has also captured what was becoming an increasingly powerful narrative. The landscape was changing dramatically and, with it, people were changing. There were now those who were comfortable with the huge scale of the changes and those for whom it was a source of anxiety and fear.

It is also interesting to see that the track in the foreground, obviously temporary while the cutting was excavated, has been constructed in two different ways. To the left, the track has been laid with transverse wooden sleepers while to the right the track has been laid on roughly square stone sleepers. This reflects the diversity in methods of railway construction at the time with techniques being adapted from wooden railways and tramways of the eighteenth and early nineteenth century.

View of the Embankment near Wolverton, during its Progress

Wolverton was decided upon as the notional halfway point between London and Birmingham and it was there that a large railway works was constructed. To house the workers the village of Wolverton was greatly expanded and much later the town of New Bradwell was founded. It was at this point that the railway crossed the wide valley of the River Ouse over what the company called 'the great Wolverton Viaduct'. This embankment ran for over 1½ miles across the valley and was the longest on the entire line.

Bourne's image of the building of the embankment for the viaduct can be hard to read at first. It is difficult to get a sense of the scale of the work. A train can be made out in the distance to the right of the image and at the head of the embankment a wagon is tipping excavated earth down the slope to move the embankment forward.

This image gives a sense of the painfully slow progress of such work and the huge requirement for men and horses to work alongside the steam locomotives.

West Side of the Viaduct over the River Ouse, near Woolverton

The viaduct over the Ouse and Tow at Wolverton was one of the architectural triumphs of the building of the railway. It is 660ft long and around 56ft high and is made up of six principal arches each with a span of 60ft; each abutment has a further four, smaller, arches.

Once more, Bourne has captured the viaduct under construction and shear legs, cranes, and scaffolding have been included, along with two examples of the centring used to form each of the principal arches. To the left the embankment is only partially constructed and it has yet to meet the abutment. Throughout Bourne's work the choice has been to show a landscape that is in the process of changing. It gives an insight into a brief period of time when, for many (particularly those who lived or worked alongside the line), the world altered beyond all expectation.

View in the Deep Cutting near Blisworth

For 1½ miles after leaving Blisworth Station the track ran through a cutting that was at times 60ft deep. The local geology meant that the work of making the cutting and ensuring a stable retaining face of rock was extremely difficult. This image captures these problems by including two large props on the left-hand side of the track.

Bourne has included a train running through the cutting, perhaps implying that the route itself was safe. It is markedly different to the trains of wagons laden with spoil from the construction process seen in previous images. It is made up of what appear to be passenger carriages with baggage cars to the rear. This image was made by Bourne in October 1838, just one month after the station at Blisworth was opened, so it would be highly plausible that he recorded one of the first passenger trains to run on the line.

The track in this image is laid with stone blocks as opposed to wooden sleepers, a less efficient form of construction, and a signalman can be seen with his flag indicating that the train was safe to proceed. The technology of railway signalling was something that developed only after some of the early lines were constructed and, regrettably, often only after serious accidents had taken place.

View of the Cutting near Blisworth

This image shows a passenger train (most likely the one seen from the rear in the previous print) making its way through the cutting outside Blisworth. To the right a mother holds back her child from the edge of the cutting while a couple, seated on blocks excavated from the cutting, hold a conversation.

The notion of the railway as a spectacle has been previously discussed but this image highlights what a remarkable thing the railway must have been to many people. While the steam locomotives would have been of great interest, the feats of engineering required to construct a railway would have been beyond the comprehension of many local residents. Over 300,000 pounds of gunpowder were required to complete just this section of the line.

This view of the viaduct over the River Nene at the town of Weedon was taken from the side of the Grand Junction Canal, which also ran upon a high embankment at this point. It cuts a clean line through the outskirts of the town and has separated a cemetery from the rest of the settlement. In the distance, to the right, can be made out the large buildings that made up the Royal Military Depot in the town.

The most complicated piece of engineering along the entire length of the line was the Kilsby Tunnel. Originally a budget of £99,000 to undertake the work was agreed on but it soon became clear that this sum would fall woefully short. At the time Bourne was producing his lithographs the total cost for the tunnel was estimated at being between £300,000 and £400,000. The tunnel ran for 2,442 yards in length and required two massive ventilation shafts to ensure a steady supply of fresh air.

This image shows a stationary steam engine with winding gear at the head of the larger ventilating shaft. This gear was used to raise and lower materials while the shaft was under construction. The engine is housed in a square timber structure and the beam is visible on the left. To the right of this is a separate boiler with a chimney beyond that.

By way of a contrast, Bourne has also included a horse gin, or winding engine, in the background to the left-hand side of the image. These were much simpler and older in design but were still an effective way to move materials into the tunnel itself.

Pumps for Draining the Kilsby Tunnel

Huge quantities of water were encountered when constructing the Kilsby Tunnel. Three pumps were installed which together raised up to 1,800 gallons every minute. All three of the pumps were worked from the same steam engine which was housed in the structure to the left of the image.

Once again, Bourne has included several horse gins in this image. The one to the right of the engine house has been captured in fascinating detail to the point where it could almost be reconstructed from his drawing. This is typical of Bourne's work. In some instances he employs a free, loose style to capture nature and picturesque scenery while, in others, he has a sharp eye for detail and meticulously records technical features that have captured his interest. Preparatory sketches for this series of lithographs show that he was fascinated with items of equipment, such as a block and tackle, and spent time capturing these along with the larger, more impressive scenes.

This image captures the rough and ready, fleeting landscape that must have surrounded the building of a large railway at the time. Only in the far right of the image is a landscape untouched by the railway included, almost as if to remind the viewer that what they were looking at was temporary.

Kilsby Tunnel – Interior View, Under a Working Shaft

Due to the complexity of constructing the Kilsby Tunnel in such problematic geology it was necessary to begin work at eighteen separate points along its length. This required the sinking of eighteen working shafts (in addition to the two ventilating shafts and other horizontal workings) to allow men and materials into the tunnel. The navvies used what they called 'skips' or large metal boxes, to lower down materials and to bring up spoil as work progressed.

This image is made more dramatic by the light coming down through the shaft and illuminating the tunnel and a skip in the process of being raised. This is not artistic licence; the atmosphere within the tunnel was recorded as being so humid that the light could be seen in a distinct column at the right time of day.

Kilsby Tunnel – Interior View, Under One of the Great Ventilating Shafts

This image shows the junction of one of the two 'great ventilating shafts' with the tunnel itself. The two ventilating shafts were 90ft and 130ft in depth respectively and required 1 million bricks to complete. In building the tunnel and the many additional shafts 1,300 men were employed and twelve steam engines were required to work both night and day.

View from above the Kilsby Tunnel

Once again, Bourne has juxtaposed the engineering works of the railway with the unspoilt countryside. To the left a couple enjoy a stroll through the wooded landscape while to the right the horse gins can be seen at work, operating above one of the many shafts sunk to enable the Kilsby Tunnel to be built.

It is unclear what the small building in the woods represents. It is perhaps one of the temporary structures that the navvies built as accommodation along the line.

These temporary camps, along with the larger more permanent ones were often the cause of anxiety for local inhabitants who saw the navvies as untrustworthy drunks and fighters; a reputation often, but not always, well earned.

RAILWAY BRIDGE _ RUGBY.

At this point along the line the railway crossed the Lutterworth Road, seen as one of the main approaches to the town of Rugby itself. This bridge was constructed in a distinctive architectural style with the deliberate aim of harmonising it with the 'scholastic buildings of Rugby' itself. It was constructed with a flat pointed cast-iron arch and decorative spandrels for the main span and octagonal towers for the main abutments. The bridge was designed by Robert Stephenson and it was widely reported that Rugby School contributed £1,000 to its construction, although apparently, this was denied by the Railway Company.

The use of historical architectural styles in the design of railway structures such as bridges and stations was to become fairly common. Certainly the GWR can be seen to have employed this concept as evidenced by Bourne in his subsequent lithographs of the line.

It is significant that the railway company wanted to fit in with the architecture it passed by. What this image shows is modernity masquerading as 'olde England', fully aware that it had, to some degree, to make concessions to the world around it.

Sherbourne Viaduct, near Coventry

After leaving Rugby and passing through the intermediate station at Brandon, the railway crossed the River Avon on a viaduct. In this image the train is an almost insignificant part of the composition and the viaduct, which was made up of nine arches, each 24ft in span, sits comfortably in the landscape. In the distance, to the left, two of the spires of the city of Coventry can be seen.

This image is a classic example of what could be called the 'Railway Pastoral'. It shows the railway settling into the English landscape. While the countryside has been altered by the coming of the railways it has not been altered beyond recognition. Allaying the anxieties of the landowning classes about the railways was undoubtedly the subtext to many of Bourne's images.

Only about a mile further along the same embankment as the previous image the railway crossed the River Sherbourne. Built of stone and iron, it crossed the river just outside the city of Coventry.

This image is far more architectural than the previous lithograph. Again, the train itself is almost insignificant but the beauty and symmetry of the viaduct has been perfectly delineated.

The banks of the Avon provided a perfect counterpoint to the clean lines of the viaduct. While the Midlands were an industrial powerhouse by the 1830s, the landscapes that the railway moved through were often dramatic and beautiful.

Almost 100 miles along the line and around 12 miles from Birmingham, the railway crossed another river, this time the Blythe. This bridge was deemed to be a 'substantial' structure at the time of its construction and one that provided a forcible contrast with the much older bridge that ran parallel to it only a few yards away.

Throughout the images Bourne produced, the railway was shown as something new but essentially settled within the landscape. Those witnessing the building of the railways in the mid-nineteenth century were aware that they were seeing history being made. Bourne has presented this idea of history in the making in this image. The old and the new bridges, one ruinous and picturesque, the other clean and classical in style, sit side by side, almost as equals while, in the centre of the image, a horse-drawn cart and a mounted man cross the river. This slightly self-deprecatory composition which places the new bridge on a par with the old footbridge can again be read as an attempt to show that the railways were not necessarily the rapacious monsters as pictured in many of the satirical sketches of the day.

Birmingham Station

After a journey of just over 112 miles the train terminated at Birmingham Curzon Street in another beautifully designed classical station, aesthetically the equal of Euston although not in terms of scale. The façade, with its distinctive four Ionic columns, housed the refreshments rooms, offices and a director's apartment. Designed by the architect Philip Hardwick, the building cost £26,000 to construct.

It was the gateway to the industrial and entrepreneurial heart of the country and was described at the time as a 'far-famed arena of art and manufacture'. By 1838, when the first drawings for this image were made, Birmingham was already criss-crossed with a large number of canals that brought in raw materials and transported finished goods to market. By linking Birmingham directly with London these goods could be moved to the capital in a fraction of the time and at a fraction of the cost.

The fact that the same architectural style was used in both Birmingham and London is significant. It points towards the railway company adopting a particular style which they felt represented its aims and ambitions. It was classical and thus reflected the solidity and timelessness of the Greek and Roman empires. It also meant that embodied in Curzon Street Station was a piece of aspirational metropolitan swagger that brought the two cities closer together both physically and culturally.

2

The Great Western Railway

The GWR, like the L&BR before it, had its roots in the early 1820s. Its initial concept was to link Bristol, then the second city of the country, with London. The notion was put forward by a group of Bristol-based merchants who were keen, for obvious financial reasons, to improve communication between the two cities. Up to this point goods were moved overland either along the roads, which were often in an extremely poor condition, or via a series of river navigations and canals. At the western end of the journey was the Avon Navigation while, at the eastern, there was the River Thames; in between there was the Wiltshire and Berkshire Canal to the north and the Kennet and Avon Canal to the south. As with all canals, journey times could be incredibly slow, particularly if weather conditions were poor, and this meant that business could be disrupted and money lost. It was hoped that a railway would lead to decreased journey times and increased carrying capacity.

In late 1824 a railway company was formed with the idea of raising £1.5 million by way of £100 shares. A route was quickly surveyed by one of the directors of the company, John Loudon Macadam, the road builder, although, curiously, this route was to stop short of London at Brentford. However, no Act of Parliament was ever sought and the idea died quietly along with many other proposed railways in that period.

It was with the opening of the Liverpool & Manchester Railway in 1830 that interest in a rail link between the two cities was reignited and by 1832 another route had been surveyed which would carry the line to the heart of London near to the Edgware Road and potentially link up with the then proposed L&BR. The name of the scheme was put forward as the Bristol & London Railway. After much lobbying on the part of influential Bristol merchants a sum of capital was raised and by March 1833 Isambard Kingdom Brunel, then only 27, had been appointed as surveyor.

The Bristol merchants, who were at the heart of the project, had spent some time drumming up support in London and by August 1833 there was a joint meeting of the London and Bristol committees, which decided upon the formation of a company with the name of the Great Western Railway.

The survey of the line led to an estimated cost of construction of £2.8 million over a length of line of approximately 120 miles. The first prospectus of the company laid out the intention to raise £3 million from the sale of shares at £100 each. Initially the shares did not sell well and there was considerable opposition to the railway from landowners along the proposed line, not least of which came from Eton College at Windsor. By July 1834 the scheme had been approved by the House of Commons (but only after a long drawn-out examining committee) but was rejected summarily by the House of Lords and the GWR had to return to planning their next move.

Undaunted by this setback, the company resurveyed the routeand revised the costs down from £2.8 million to £2.5 million. Once more the scheme was submitted to the House of Commons, where it was eventually passed without opposition. In the House of Lords, despite concerns over running trains on a Sunday, the safety of the planned Box Tunnel and the moral well-being of the students at Eton College, the bill was eventually passed. The GWR received royal assent on 31 August 1835.

As it stood, the line that received assent was planned to join the L&BR, by then under construction, at Kensall Green. This was a concern to Brunel who already had in mind the idea of constructing the railway on a much wider gauge than that adopted by the Stephensons. The L&BR was built to a gauge of 4ft 8½in while Brunel advocated a gauge of 7ft ¼in. By linking in with an existing railway his plans to use what was quickly to become known as the Broad Gauge would be impossible. However, talks with the L&BR proved extremely difficult and were eventually broken off; by August 1836 the GWR had secured land, and the necessary permissions, for a station at Paddington in the heart of London.

While Brunel was always convinced of the advantages of the Broad Gauge there was considerable concern from both without and within the company. However, after a vote of shareholders and the examination of the line by eminent engineers the Broad Gauge was officially adopted by the GWR. Construction of the railway began almost immediately after receiving royal assent. Although Brunel had an able staff of surveyors there is evidence to suggest that he oversaw most aspects of the construction himself and his letters point toward him travelling along the route of the line frequently.

The building of the railway was let out in a series of contracts and the first part of the line, that between London and Farringdon Road, was opened in stages between June 1838 and July 1840. At the same time, work had commenced at the western end of the line and the line from Bristol to Bath opened to the public in late August 1840. Between Farringdon Road and Bath the builders were plagued with bad weather and heavy soils and work was difficult and slow. In addition to this, the construction of Box Tunnel delayed things considerably. Once opened, the railway was virtually level through its entire length – testament to the skills and perseverance of Brunel as an engineer and a feature which later led to the sobriquet of 'Brunel's billiard table'.

The line was opened from London to Bristol on 30 June 1841 and the directors of the company, riding in the first train from London, arrived in Bristol in only four hours. By canal the journey would have taken between seven and ten days and, when conditions were poor, this could increase to weeks, or even months. By August 1847 this journey time had been cut again and was only two hours and forty-three minutes.

However, the building of the GWR came at a price; in total the railway had cost over £6.1 million, a staggering increase from the £2.5 million included in the bill that received royal assent. But the railway quickly started to flourish and in its first few years of operation began to acquire a whole series of other, smaller railways in the region. A characteristic that was to remain a key facet of the GWR's identity, the takeover of other lines, was evident even in the early years of operation.

Bourne's lithographs of the GWR under construction have a more mature feel to those produced of the L&BR but, once again, he captured the lived experience of a railway being carved out through the landscape. His work on this railway was undoubtedly more sophisticated but its beauty is undeniable.

Wharncliffe Viaduct, Hanwell

The Wharncliffe Viaduct was described as 'the largest piece of brickwork' along the entire length of the GWR as it was first conceived. It was built just outside of Hanwell, only 7 miles from London. It was named after Lord Wharncliffe who was a staunch supporter of the railway and presided over the committee in the House of Lords which approved the original proposals.

The viaduct was 900ft long and crossed the Vale of the Brent. Designed by Brunel, the viaduct was built by the partnership of Grissell and Peto. It was one of the first major pieces of construction to be undertaken along the line.

Bourne's image is striking and shows the influence of ancient Egyptian architecture in the piers. It is interesting to note, throughout the railway, how medieval, classical and Egyptian styles of building were adopted. It perhaps lent the structures an air of history which they would otherwise have lacked.

Again, as with many of the earlier images, traditional farming practices have been included alongside the railway. Cattle are resting in the shade of the viaduct while hay is being gathered in and loaded onto horse-drawn wagons.

Bridge over the Uxbridge Road, near Hanwell

The railway, as with so many others constructed at the time, was built in a landscape that was already crossed by rivers, canals and roads. Each of these had to be negotiated and their rights of way respected. The bridge over the Uxbridge Road is just one example of how this was achieved.

The bridge was a complex structure consisting of cast-iron girders and brick and cement arches and, in this image, it appears as a remarkably geometric structure.

A train, hauling both freight and passengers, can just be seen passing over the bridge while, below, people go about their business apparently unaffected by the railway. It is hard to imagine exactly what impact the appearance of structures like these had on the landscape and in the imagination of those who witnessed such change. Bourne's lithographs are a record of just how much the railways remade the English countryside.

The quality of Bourne's draughtsmanship is always on show in his lithographs. His images of the GWR are more mature and sophisticated than those of the L&BR that he produced just a few years before. But it is important to note that the railway builders themselves had become more confident and sophisticated in this short time.

Slough Station was only 18 miles from Paddington and, due to its proximity to Windsor, was regularly used by Queen Victoria. The Royal Hotel benefitted from the association with the monarch and was considered to be particularly well fitted out with furniture taken from the state rooms of the French palaces of Louis XIV and XV.

This image shows the Queen arriving at the station with her retinue. The GWR was keen to overcome the anxieties that many people, particularly landowners, had regarding the potential for disruption that the railway might bring. By picturing Queen Victoria about to undertake a railway journey Bourne was perhaps implying some form of royal assent which would undoubtedly have had a positive influence on many who had their misgivings about this new form of transport.

The Maidenhead Bridge

When the GWR first opened in June 1838 it only ran for 22½ miles from Paddington Station in London to Maidenhead Station. It was only in July 1839 that the line was opened for traffic beyond this point.

Just past the station the railway crossed the River Thames by means of the Maidenhead Bridge. This bridge was the source of much speculation at the time due to the fact that it only made use of two spans to cross more than 250ft of river. The arches were particularly flat which led to many commentators suggesting that the bridge would be dangerously unstable.

The design of the bridge was dictated by the existence of a single bank of stable geology within the centre of the river that provided good foundations for the pier and the fact that the river, one of the busiest waterways in the country, had to remain navigable for barges and other traffic. Once completed the bridge was considered a success not just in terms of its engineering but also as a thing of beauty. Bourne's image shows the entire length of the bridge with its abutments partially obscured by trees; a classic practice used to introduce a touch of the picturesque into the scene. The train itself is small and almost insignificant in scale.

In 1844 J.M.W. Turner painted his famous picture *Rain, Steam and Speed – The Great Western Railway*, showing a train travelling over the Maidenhead Bridge. It is interesting to compare the two images. Bourne's lithograph has a sense of calm, classical composure about it, whereas Turner captured a sense of dynamism and vitality.

Sonning Cutting

After leaving Maidenhead the railway left behind the gravels of London and ran through a landscape of chalk and clay. It passed through the village of Twyford, Wiltshire, which was, from July 1839 until March 1840, the terminus of the railway only some 30 miles from London. Beyond this a series of cuttings were excavated which removed the need for a costly and potentially problematic tunnel. The Sonning Cutting was almost 2 miles long and, as well as removing the need for a tunnel, bypassed the village of Sonning itself where locals objected to having the railway running so close.

The text that accompanies Bourne's lithographs, published in 1846, was keen to point out the quantities of material that were excavated and the skill used in the construction of the cutting. However, even at the time of writing, the Sonning Cutting was perhaps better known for the accident which occurred on Christmas Eve 1841. Heavy rains caused part of the cutting to slip onto the line which was then hit by an oncoming train. The train was arranged with the freight wagons to the rear which, on impact, crushed the passenger carriages which were directly behind the locomotive. Eight passengers were killed at the time and many more were seriously injured, one of whom later died.

Pangbourne Station

The railway ran through several large towns along its route from London to Bristol and, after leaving the Sonning Cutting, went through Reading. However, it is interesting to note that no image of Reading or its station was published. Instead there is a deliberate focus on the more minor, or 'second class' stations such as that at Pangbourne, just over 40 miles from London.

The station was built in what was called an 'Elizabethan style' with a small station building and two covered platforms. A short distance from the station was located a yard with turntables and accommodation for cattle. Bourne's image is very much one of a small country station at work. Alongside the well-dressed ladies and gentlemen can be seen a man in a smock-frock. Such traditional clothing was worn by farmers and those living and working in the countryside and was seen as something of a symbol of the rural poor. As early as the 1820s certain writers were saddened by how far the wearing of the smock-frock had died out and blamed this on the growing industrialisation of the countryside.

It is perhaps significant that Bourne has included visual clues as to the mixed status of those using the railway. The railways, while fundamentally engaged in the business of providing good returns for their shareholders, very often saw themselves as champions of public good where their undertakings had the potential to improve the lives of everyone, regardless of their class or status.

Bassildon Bridge over the Thames

Two bridges were constructed within 2 miles of each other to carry the railway over the River Thames, one at Basildon and the other at Moulsford. Both bridges, essentially built to the same design, were of red brick and composed of four arches each of 62ft in span. Bourne's image of the bridge at Basildon (spelled 'Bassildon' on the title of the lithograph) shows how elegant these structures were and how well they sat within the landscape.

Again, rather than show the bridge in its entirety Bourne has broken up the edges of the composition with trees, helping to embed it in the countryside. The river traffic pictured here indicates how important the Thames was as a main artery of commerce. It is likely that the horses on the right-hand riverbank had been used for hauling barges upstream as the front three are in harnesses.

Like many of the bridges and structures designed and built by Brunel, this bridge still survives on the main line from London to Bristol. Now known as the Gatehampton Bridge, it remains almost unchanged after 175 years.

Engine House, Swindon

Swindon is now well known as a railway town but it has its origins in the Anglo-Saxon period. The coming of the canals in the early 1800s led to its initial expansion but the arrival of the GWR saw it grow beyond all recognition.

The town of Swindon was 77 miles from London and just over 41 from Bristol and so was decided upon as ideally placed to build a depot for the railway along with a passenger station. In the 1840s, when it was pictured by Bourne, the main engine shed was 490 by 72ft in size and had four lines running into it capable of housing forty-eight locomotives and their tenders. This was designed to hold engines that were either in steam or could be put into steam relatively quickly. In addition to this were a number of other buildings where locomotives undergoing light repairs could

be worked on as well as engineering facilities for completely rebuilding engines. The works at Swindon were continually expanded and rebuilt and were an important part of the modern railway infrastructure up to their closure in 1986.

Bourne's view inside the engine house, where light repairs were undertaken, is a fascinating behind-the-scenes insight into a working railway in the early 1840s. It shows a locomotive being moved onto a moving platform, known as a traverser, which allowed access to the parallel rows of tracks within the shed. While it is evident that he studied the locomotives themselves, his eye for architectural detail is exceptional. The construction techniques used on the building can be easily seen and, indeed, it feels as if the engine house could be rebuilt from this drawing alone.

In the main, Bourne's lithographs of the GWR show a working railway. In this sense they differ greatly from his images of the L&BR which were often of a railway being built. However, in this image of the line at Wootton Bassett (now Royal Wootton Bassett) a gang of men can be seen packing ballast on the line.

To the left can be seen a signalman standing outside of his small shelter. The signal itself is just to the left of the box and comprises a horizontal bar which moved the rails across and a disc which, when visible to the driver of the locomotive, would indicate that it was safe to proceed. When the GWR opened to traffic as far as Maidenhead in 1838 there had been no provision for set signalling along the line. It was assumed that the company's own police, who each patrolled a set piece of track, would be able to control the trains using hand signals alone. It was quickly found that this was not the case. The development of ever safer methods of managing trains on the line to safeguard against collisions was often something that developed directly out of studying the causes of accidents on the railway.

Chippenham

Chippenham station was just over 98 miles from London and just 24 from Bristol. This section of line was opened in May 1841, and the arrival of the first public train was celebrated by the mayor, Brunel and several of the company's directors with a public breakfast in the town. The railway entered the town on an embankment that gave fine views of the town itself.

Bourne's view shows the town, with its church spire and the outlying meadows, almost as if from the footplate of a locomotive. It is a 'driver's eye view' that would have been a very novel perspective in the early 1840s.

The 13 miles of line that lay between Chippenham and Bath comprised some of the most complicated and involved engineering on the entire railway. The largest undertaking was undoubtedly the construction of Box Tunnel, which at just under 2 miles in length was the longest in the country at the time. It was dug in six sections and required six ventilating shafts each 25ft in diameter.

The tunnel was begun in 1836 and opened in June 1841. During this time around 1,100 men and over 100 horses were engaged in the work; for the final six months it is recorded that a total of 4,000 men and 300 horses were taken on to complete the project. The navvies who dug the tunnel apparently spent a great deal of their time, when not working, engaged in drinking and fighting in the local villages. Once completed, the navvies moved on, much to the rejoicing of the local inhabitants.

At its western end, Box Tunnel opened out into a deep cutting where the portal was flanked with large retaining walls. The portal was designed by Brunel in a classical style and had the feel of an ornamental bridge that might not look out of place in the landscaped grounds of a stately home.

In this image the signalman and his signal can be seen indicating a clear line to the approaching train while, above, can be seen farmers gathering hay on to a wagon.

The inclusion of such rural practices reinforces the idea of a planned landscape where the railway sits harmoniously alongside the older, established ways.

It has been suggested that Brunel designed the tunnel along an alignment that would allow the rising sun to be visible along its length on his birthday, 9 April, each year. While an interesting story, there is no evidence that this is true.

View from above the Tunnel, Box

Bourne's background and training as an engraver of landscapes is clear in this image of the landscape above and beyond Box Tunnel. The rugged rocks and wind-blown trees on the summit of Hazelbury Hill have all the elements of the sublime and the picturesque which prized 'roughness' over clean, smooth lines. However, Bourne has been careful to include the straight lines of the railway as it cut across the landscape and into Middle Hill Tunnel in the distance. By combining the aesthetics of the eighteenth-century landscape engravers and his keenly observed studies of the railway, Bourne began to create an entirely new set of values, values that prized the beauty and simplicity of the modern and industrial as much as the old and traditional.

Once again, the scale of the railway in this image is significant. The focus is mainly on the countryside itself with the railway included as an addition, or perhaps, ornament to it. By placing the railway into a rural context Bourne began the process of what one writer has referred to as 'domesticating the railway dragon'. Today nothing could be considered as more quintessentially English than a steam railway running through the countryside but in the 1840s it required some effort for many to appreciate its aesthetic merits.

Bathford Bridge

The bridge over the River Avon at Bathford was considered to be 'perfectly plain' but also 'one of the most beautiful on the line'. This appreciation of the simplicity and elegance of the bridge's single 54ft span shows the confidence that the railway company had, both in their designer, Brunel, and in their project as a whole.

In some way, the fact that an image of this simple bridge has been included is an example of how the GWR wanted to integrate quality of design throughout the railway. This is in much the same vein as the inclusion of Pangbourne Station over one of the larger stations at, for example, Reading.

Once more, the overall impression is one of an eighteenth-century landscaped estate. In the foreground the cattle have come down to the water's edge while in the background the village of Bathford nestles in between Farley and Claverton Downs. The bridge is a well-thought-through addition to the landscape; an addition that might have been seen to improve the view in the same sense that the building of a romantic folly might.

Bath Hampton

Running between the River Avon and the Kennet and Avon Canal, the railway passed close by the village of Bathampton (then spelled Bath Hampton). This provided Bourne with the opportunity to produce one of his most striking images. To the left the parish church, surrounded by cattle and locals leaning against stable doors, is a symbol of everything that is settled and stable while, to the right, the railway runs, straight as an arrow, cutting a swathe through the landscape. All that separates these two worlds is a low fence and some trees. But they are seen coexisting peacefully – so much so that the cattle are comfortable enough to lie down on the grassy bank to the side of the railway.

Much could be said about the constant appearance of churches in the railway landscapes of Bourne. In reality, the line does not run quite as close to the church as Bourne's image suggests; the composition has been constructed so as to derive maximum impact from the juxtaposition between the old and the new. Bourne has deliberately shaped the landscape to ensure that these two worlds can be pictured together. The authority of the Church, while perhaps threatened by the pace of industrial development and the social change that it brought with it, is not being challenged by the railway. The image clearly shows how the railway wanted to be seen as respecting, and adding to, the older order of things.

Railway and Avon near Bath

Bath is considered to be the finest Georgian city in England and was already an established tourist attraction and holiday location in the nineteenth century. In this image the train is viewed from the rear as it makes its way towards the town. It is an unusual perspective but it allows the viewer to see the last vehicle which appears to be a flat wagon with a barouche or similar horse-drawn carriage loaded on top.

In the early years of the railways it was common practice for the more wealthy passengers to have their personal horse-drawn vehicle mounted directly onto railway wagons so that, once at their chosen station, they could continue to their final destination without inconvenience.

Sydney Gardens – Bath

It was important to the GWR that when the line reached Bath the beauty of the city was not in any way damaged. The railway arrived by cutting through Sydney Gardens, a pleasure garden complex laid out in the last years of the eighteenth century. The company was keen to ensure that the landscaping of the line was 'arranged so as to increase, rather than injure, the attractions of the gardens'.

Two bridges were built to reconnect the two halves of the gardens and the embankment was built with a long, low parapet that allowed those in the gardens to view the railway. Overall it gave the effect of a long ha-ha which transformed the railway itself into something of a tourist spectacle, to be looked at and remarked upon. This is in marked contrast to the instances where railways had to be buried in tunnels or deep cuttings because landowners did not want to see them.

Bath

There are several lithographs of Bath included in Bourne's volume of the GWR, more than both London and Bristol, which indicates the importance given it by the company and the artist.

The railway came into Bath at some elevation and, having emerged from the cutting through Sydney Gardens, it can be seen running along a high embankment into the heart of the town. The line as far as Bath was opened in June 1841 and

Bourne has chosen to show the line either under partial reconstruction or repair. A gang of workmen are unloading large timbers, presumably the longitudinal sleepers used in the laying of broad-gauge track, while a small group of foremen discuss business. In the distance, the elegant buildings of Bath rise up out of the trees, while to the right can be seen the cast-iron bridge used to carry the railway over the Avon.

St James's Bridge and Station, Bath

Before entering the station the line again crossed the Avon by way of the St James's Bridge. Building this skew-arch bridge was challenging as it was washed away in heavy flooding when almost complete and had to be rebuilt from scratch. It is an elegant classical structure with protruding quoins and keystones. Built, naturally, out of Bath stone, it was very much in keeping with the architecture of the town.

At its western end the bridge ran almost directly into the station embankment and the station buildings can be seen to the right of this image. Signals and a water tower have been included just before the station building itself. The station, which was said at the time to have been designed in the style of 'James I with debased Gothic windows and Romanesque ornaments' shows, perhaps, how playful railway architects could be in designing their buildings. To have picked three distinct architectural styles spanning around 600 years is evidence of the creativity and influences of Brunel.

Bath Station

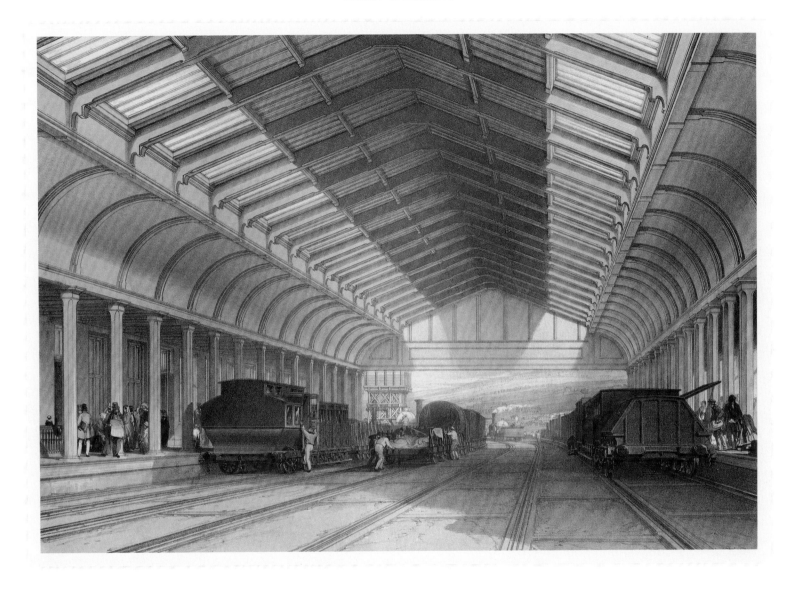

Apart from its eclectic mix of architectural styles, the station at Bath was noteworthy due to its unusual roof construction. It had a span of 60ft but did not make use of any buttresses or ties. Instead it was built using large beams which, springing from the upright columns and acting almost like the arms of cranes, met in the middle of the roof. While this was undoubtedly an elegant solution to the problem of roofing such a large space it did mean that the supporting columns were only 4ft away from the platform edge and thus were somewhat inconvenient for passengers when getting on and off the trains.

In this image Bourne has captured a busy principal station at work. There were four roads into the station, with the outside two being used for regular traffic and the inside two being mainly used as sidings. Bourne has not only paid a great deal of attention to the structure of the station but also to the vehicles themselves. To the left can be seen a 'posting carriage' with a clerestory roof. These were effectively the saloon cars of their day and were said to have been 'fitted up in a style of elegance not met with in any other railway-conveyance in the Kingdom (save only the royal railway-carriage)'.

Oblique Wooden Bridge, Bath

Bath lay just under 11 miles from the GWR terminus at Bristol. At the time this journey took just over thirty minutes. After leaving Bath Station the railway once again crossed the Avon. This time it was carried by a wooden bridge on such a skew to the river that although the distance from bank to bank was only 80ft the total length of the bridge was more than 160ft.

The design of this bridge reflects the character of the buildings around it, which in Bourne's image present more of a medieval townscape than the familiar Georgian one. The river is shown as a busy commercial waterway with barges and small boats either loaded with goods or, as in the case with the small boat to the left of the scene, towing a load of timber.

Once more, this is a clear sign of the lengths to which the railway went to harmonise with the surrounding land- and townscapes through which it ran.

Twerton near Bath

Once out of the city Bourne's images take on a familiar picturesque quality again. This view, taken from the high ground just about a mile outside of Bath, shows the railway running alongside both the main road and the River Avon. Including these other forms of transport in this image is another way in which Bourne could help to settle the railway into the landscape.

A large amount of the village of Twerton (referred to as Twiverton in the accompanying text) was demolished to allow the line to pass through the land. This was made possible by wealthy industrialist and local landowner Mr Charles Wilkins. Just beyond the castellated arch that crosses the railway can be seen a large series of buildings; these are the cloth mills owned by Wilkins and which provided employment for a large number of the village inhabitants.

Avon and Railway, Fox's Wood

At this point in the journey Bristol is only a few miles distant and the line continues to run alongside the Avon which, in parts, had to be diverted to allow the engineers enough land to excavate a shelf into the hillside for the trackbed.

To the left can be seen a barge and a small wharf with a community of houses. There were considerable coal measures in this area and large quantities of coal and coke were shipped downstream to Bristol. The train, running above the river, appears to be the same one pictured coming in to Bath as it is possible to make out a barouche on the flat wagon at the rear.

As the railway ran below Fox's Wood it entered a series of short tunnels, known officially as tunnels Nos 1, 2 and 3. It was during the excavations for these tunnels that a number of archaeological finds were unearthed, including a Roman villa complete with mosaic.

Tunnel No. 3 was also known as the 'long tunnel' due to the fact that, at 1,017 yards long, it was almost three times longer than either of the other two tunnels along that stretch of line. Excavating this tunnel was both difficult and time consuming.

In this image Bourne has shown the east entrance to the tunnel which initially ran through a gallery of hewn rock. The tunnel was cut through rock that was considered to be stable enough to dispense with brickwork and, for its entire length, when first opened, the living rock made up both the sides and roof of the tunnel.

Bourne shows the scale of the undertaking in this image with a group of navvies working away at the rock face. It is interesting, from a contemporary perspective, to see the total absence of safety equipment available to the workmen who stand at the top of the rocky outcrop without any ropes or harnesses.

Long Tunnel – Fox's Wood, from the West

This image shows the entrance to the long tunnel as it would have been seen approaching from Bristol. Brunel made great use of medieval design and influences in his railway structures and this is no exception.

To the left the Avon is busy with barges unloading material for the construction work. There appears to be a large supply of timber on the hillside to the left of the tunnel which could well have been used for supports and props in the manner seen directly to the right of the tunnel mouth. Records show that Brunel relied heavily on the river to bring building materials to the sites of construction.

This image shows the west front of No. 2 Tunnel in an incomplete state. In the eighteenth century the writer William Gilpin suggested that the quality of Tintern Abbey might be significantly improved with the judicious use of a mallet. In other words, the more rough and ruinous a thing was the more beautiful it became. It is tempting to suppose that Brunel was thinking along similar lines when this tunnel front was left unfinished; it, perhaps, added a certain historical charm to the structure. Certainly, the commentary that accompanied this illustration recorded the ruinous state of this structure as producing a 'very serviceable, and … picturesque tunnel front'.

Sadly, the truth is somewhat more prosaic. Extremely wet weather in the winter and spring of 1840 led to work slipping behind schedule and to several masonry structures being condemned. This meant that the tunnel front was not completed on time. However, the wet weather continued and brought down a section of the embankment which removed the structural need to complete the tunnel front and the planned retaining wall that went alongside it. The structure remained in this attractively decrepit state for over fifty years.

Just before entering the city of Bristol the railway once more crossed the Avon, this time over a bridge in the Gothic style; it was thought that such a style was an appropriate complement to the buildings and character of the ancient city of Bristol. The main span of the bridge is 100ft in length.

The train crossing the bridge is worthy of note. It clearly shows a covered goods wagon, two passenger carriages and then further goods wagons to the rear.

This would have been contrary to the recommendations made after the second inquest into the accident at Sonning Cutting which stated that passenger carriages should be placed further away from the locomotive to ensure that they would not be crushed by heavy goods wagons in the event of an accident.

Bristol

In this wide view of the city of Bristol the bridge over the Avon can be seen again, to the right of the picture. It helps to provide some context for a structure that in the previous image appeared to rise up from the ground.

As in previous lithographs by Bourne the composition is one designed to emphasise contrast; but in this case it is not so much the modern railway and the ancient church or village. It is a contrast between the activities of the countryside and the activities of the urban environment. In the foreground men can be seen felling and limbing trees, possibly to be used as construction material for the railway. In the background the chimneys of the factories and works of Bristol can be seen. It is perhaps simplistic to talk in terms of rural and urban as they were both closely interrelated, but this image shows the impact of the rapid growth of the towns and cities on the wider landscape. The more traditional practices of the woodsman were, in the 1840s, being carried out with a view of chimneys and coal smoke as opposed to forest and field.

Bristol Goods Shed

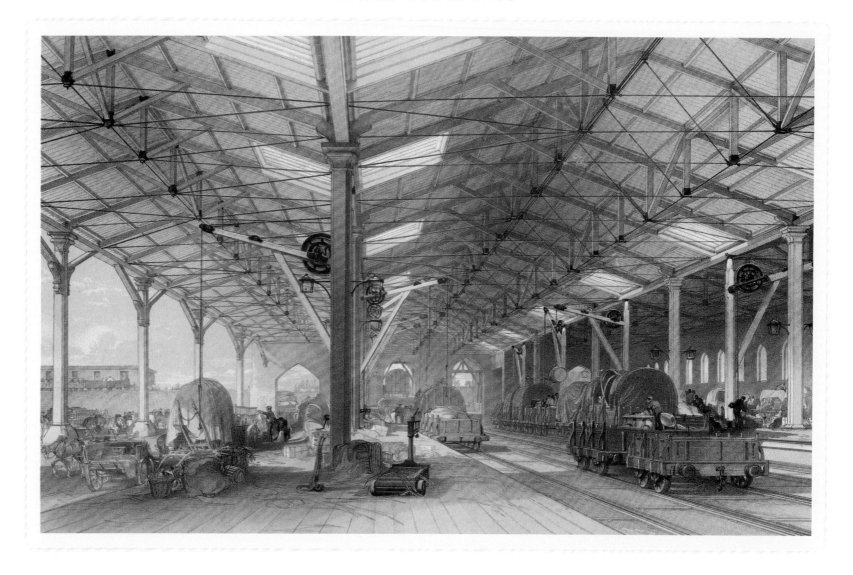

Bourne once again shows his architectural prowess in this image of the goods shed at Bristol. The complex arrangement of tie bars radiating out from the roof trusses create a lattice-like effect supporting a roof that originally spanned three sets of rails. In total, when first built, the goods shed was more than 300ft long and 130ft wide and accommodated three turntables.

The image shows a busy terminus with goods coming into and out of the station on horse-drawn carts and wagons. There were a row of cranes attached to the main columns in the building that were used to load and unload the wagons; these can be seen on both sides of the shed, suggesting that one side (the right) was dedicated to goods coming into Bristol and the other (the left) goods going out.

In the background of this image can be seen a piece of machinery that was peculiar to Bristol goods shed. The level of the rails in the shed was around 12ft below that of the main line coming into the station; this was, one assumes, to facilitate loading and unloading. This necessitated the construction of a pair of hydraulic slings, or 'scales' as they were termed, which raised and lowered the wagons on entering or leaving the shed. This piece of machinery was capable of lifting a load of 10 tons in weight.

Bristol Station

At the end of the 118-mile journey the trains of Brunel's GWR pulled into Bristol Station, known more commonly as Bristol Temple Meads. Built of Bath stone between 1839 and 1841, the design was inspired by the architecture of the Elizabethan period. Within three years of its opening, two other railways, the Bristol & Exeter and the Bristol & Gloucester, both designed by Brunel, were operating out of the station.

The image shows the remarkable decorative hammer-beam type roof. In actuality the roof was constructed in a similar fashion to that of Bath, with the principal beams springing from the columns like the arms of a crane and meeting in the middle. As with the station at Bath, it is likely that the columns were a similar inconvenience to passengers.

Bourne shows five lines coming into the station and the image has a particularly accurate depiction of a locomotive. Very often, the locomotives in Bourne's images are almost incidental, running at speed through a landscape that dwarfs them. In this image can be seen one of the 2-2-2 locomotives that the GWR used in the early years of operation.

Postscript

The proposing of new railways reached a peak in the mid 1840s. The Railway Mania and the crash that followed it saw the dreams of many speculators and investors (along with one or two would-be directors) abruptly ended. But, out of the wreckage, there were still many proposed lines that had been based on a sound financial basis and that met a clear need. It was these projects that would go on to be built. In a sense, the bursting of the railway bubble served an important function insofar as it stress-tested the lines that had been proposed and many that were found wanting were abandoned.

But the excitement and energy of that first phase of railway building had, to some degree, abated and the pioneering spirit of the railways had been tempered by a newfound caution. Bourne had been present at a period of unprecedented fervour and had seen the landscape transformed before his eyes. At first he drew the railways because they excited him, but later he was officially commissioned to document their construction and operation. His lithographs were not only beautiful and informative but were, to some degree, political. Of course, there were arguments about capital costs, efficiencies, the rate of return on shares and the impact on a landowners' hunting to be taken into account but Bourne's work showed how a railway could be a thing of beauty. His lithographs documented a series of changes in the landscape of England and attempted to show that these changes did not necessarily have to be something to fear.

Bourne continued to document great industrial building projects into the middle of the nineteenth century. In 1847 he travelled to what was then Russia with the engineer Charles Blacker Vignoles and captured the construction of the bridge over the Dneiper at Kiev. He spent many years in Russia and illustrated two volumes of a book called *Life in Russia* in 1848, possibly while back in England. Vignoles' diaries record that Bourne had become interested in photography and was taking daguerreotypes of both natural and man-made phenomena. Bourne returned to England in 1852 where he continued to pursue his photographic interests.

While there are some watercolours and drawings, often of maritime scenes, known to be by Bourne, little is known about his work through the latter half of the nineteenth century. Records show that in 1866 he married a young woman called Catherine Cripps and settled in a home in Teddington, Middlesex. He attempted three times to become a member of the New Watercolour Society between 1866 and 1877 only to be rejected on each occasion. His death certificate from February 1896 records him simply as 'Artist (painter)'.

It seems poignant that a man who captured the spirit of the early railway builders with such verve and vigour should end his life with rejection and relative obscurity. There is always a sense that quality work should be rewarded with lasting posterity but there is little evidence to suggest that this was the case.

It is, however, always worth ending on a positive note. Bourne's lithographs of the building of the L&BR and GWR had a lasting impact. They helped to naturalise the railway, a relative newcomer, into the landscapes of England. That a preserved steam railway operating on a quiet branch line is still considered to be something quintessentially English is, in no small part, due to his influence. On top of this, there is much more by way of research that is needed to understand his later life and his experiments with photography. It may be that, at some point in the future, his full influence will be far better understood, but until that time we can enjoy these lithographs with pleasure.